Being a U.S. Citizen

RULES AND LAWS IN THE UNITED STATES

By Charlotte Taylor

Enslow PUBLISHING

DISCOVER!

Please visit our website, www.enslow.com. For a free color catalog of all our high-quality books, call toll free 1-800-398-2504 or fax 1-877-980-4454.

Library of Congress Cataloging-in-Publication Data

Names: Taylor, Charlotte, 1978– author.
Title: Rules and laws in the United States / Charlotte Taylor.
Description: New York : Enslow Publishing, 2021. | Series: Being a U.S. citizen | Includes index.
Identifiers: LCCN 2019056200 | ISBN 9781978517530 (library binding) | ISBN 9781978517516 (paperback) | ISBN 9781978517523 (6 Pack) | ISBN 9781978517547 (ebook)
Subjects: LCSH: Rule of law—United States—Juvenile literature.
Classification: LCC KF382 .T39 2020 | DDC 340/.11—dc23
LC record available at https://lccn.loc.gov/2019056200

Published in 2021 by
Enslow Publishing
101 West 23rd Street, Suite #240
New York, NY 10011

Designer: Laura Bowen
Editor: Megan Quick

Photo credits: Cover, pp. 1, 16, 18, 20 MicroOne/Shutterstock.com; pp. 4, 8 ann131313/Shutterstock.com; p. 5 ZoranOrcik/Shutterstock.com; p. 6 StockVector/Shutterstock.com; p. 7 Hafiez Razali/Shutterstock.com; p. 9 Wavebreakmedia/iStock.com; p. 10 Vaskina mat/Shutterstock.com; p. 11 FatCamera/E+/Getty Images; p. 13 (main) Yobro10/iStock.com; p. 13 (quill) Alfmaler/Shutterstock.com; p. 14 momoforsale/Shutterstock.com; p. 15 manonallard/E+/Getty Images; p. 17 Mark Reinstein/Contributor/Corbis News/Getty Images; p. 19 donald_gruener/iStock/Getty Images Plus/Getty Images; p. 21 SDI Productions/E+Getty Images.

Portions of this work were originally authored by Ellen Ripley and published as *What Are Rules and Laws?* All new material in this edition was authored by Charlotte Taylor.

Printed in the United States of America

CPSIA compliance information: Batch #BS20ENS: For further information contact Enslow Publishing, New York, New York, at 1-800-398-2504.

CONTENTS

Boldface words appear in Words to Know.

RULES ARE FOR EVERYONE

Kids have to follow lots of rules. There are rules at school and at home. But rules are not just for kids! Adults follow rules too. Some rules are laws. Rules and laws tell us what we can and can't do. They keep us safe.

RULES CAN BE MADE BY PEOPLE LIKE YOUR MOM OR DAD. LAWS ARE MADE BY A GROUP OF LEADERS.

RULES OF THE HOUSE

Do you have many rules at home? Your **parents** may tell you when to go to bed. They may tell you not to talk to strangers. Rules help you to do the right thing. They can also keep you from getting hurt.

YOUR PARENTS GIVE YOU A BEDTIME SO YOU GET ENOUGH REST.

SCHOOL RULES

Rules are everywhere at school! They help keep things fair for everyone. Your teacher tells you to raise your hand before you speak in class. This gives everyone a fair chance. It also shows you **respect** your teacher and other **students**.

RAISING YOUR HAND IN CLASS LETS EVERYONE HAVE A TURN TO SPEAK.

PLAYING BY THE RULES

Before you play a game, you have to know the rules. Sometimes, there are a lot of rules! Having rules keeps everything fair. In sports, rules can keep you safe. Everyone can have fun when they play by the rules.

A GOOD SPORT ALWAYS FOLLOWS THE RULES.

WHAT IS A LAW?

There are important rules that all people must follow. These rules are called laws. The **government** makes laws. Some laws are for one state. Other laws are for the whole country. If people do not follow laws, they can get into big trouble.

THE U.S. CONSTITUTION IS A SET OF LAWS FOR OUR COUNTRY.

WHY DO WE HAVE LAWS?

Laws help keep order in our towns and in our country. Some laws make sure everyone is treated fairly. Other laws keep us from getting hurt. One law says that every car should have seat belts. This law keeps everyone safe.

EVERY STATE HAS A LAW THAT SAYS SMALL CHILDREN MUST RIDE IN A CAR SEAT.

FROM BILL TO LAW

A law starts as a bill. A person in the government writes the bill. The bill explains why we need a law. The leaders in **Congress** read the bill. They spend lots of time talking about it. They decide if they like the bill or not.

IT CAN TAKE MANY YEARS FOR CONGRESS TO VOTE ON A BILL.

The leaders have a vote about the bill. If more than half of the leaders vote yes, the bill passes. Then it goes to the president. He reads it and decides if he likes it. If he likes it, he signs the bill. It becomes a law.

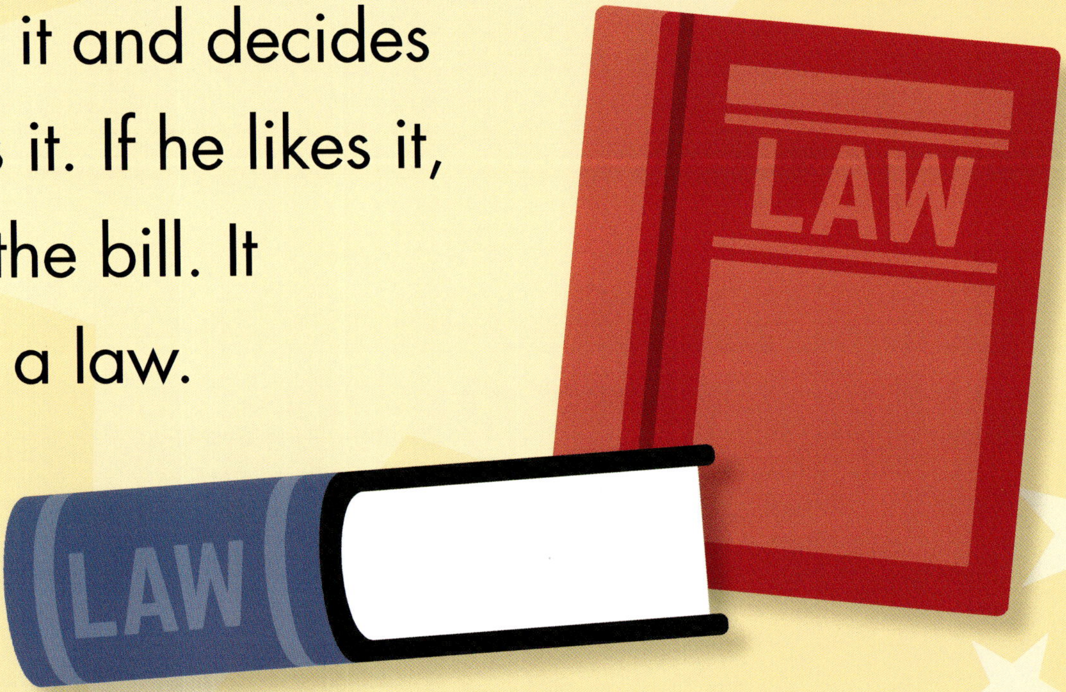

IF A PRESIDENT SAYS NO TO A BILL, IT'S CALLED A VETO.

DO THE RIGHT THING

Following rules and laws helps you to be a good person. It also helps you to be a good member of your community. Following rules and laws helps everyone in a community live together in peace.

POLICE OFFICERS MAKE SURE EVERYONE IN A COMMUNITY FOLLOWS THE LAW.

WORDS TO KNOW

Congress The part of the U.S. government that makes the laws.

government The group of people who make decisions for a city, state, or country.

parent A mother or father.

respect A feeling that someone is important and should be treated in a fair way.

student A person who goes to school or takes a class.

FOR MORE INFORMATION

Books

Cavell-Clarke, Steffi. *Respecting Rules and Laws.* New York, NY: Crabtree Publishing, 2018.

Smith, Molly. *I Can Follow the Rules.* New Rochelle, NY: Newmark Learning, 2019.

Websites

How Laws Are Made

www.ducksters.com/history/us_government/how_laws_are_made.php

Follow along on a bill's journey to become a law.

U.S. Constitution

usconstitution.net/constkidsK.html

Find out more about the Constitution and what's in it.

Publisher's note to educators and parents: Our editors have carefully reviewed these websites to ensure that they are suitable for students. Many websites change frequently, however, and we cannot guarantee that a site's future contents will continue to meet our high standards of quality and educational value. Be advised that students should be closely supervised whenever they access the internet.

INDEX